# Under My Bed

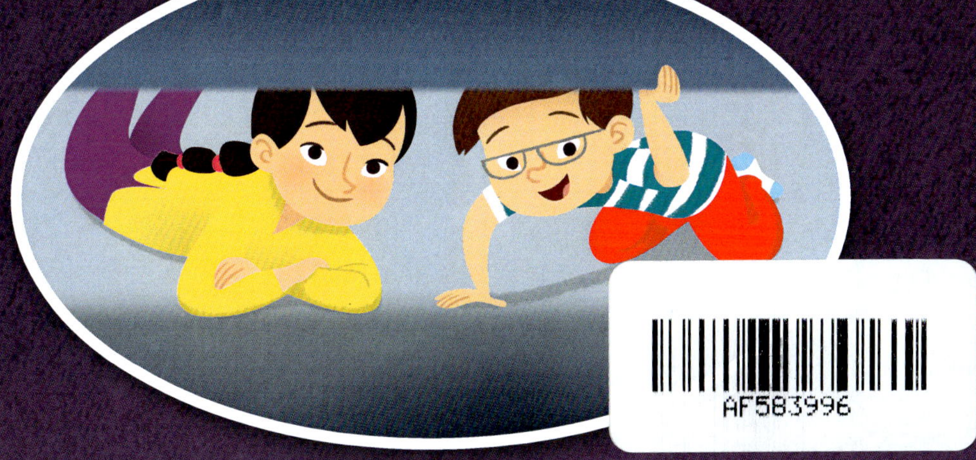



Written by Sarah Russell

Illustrated by Leigh Hedstrom

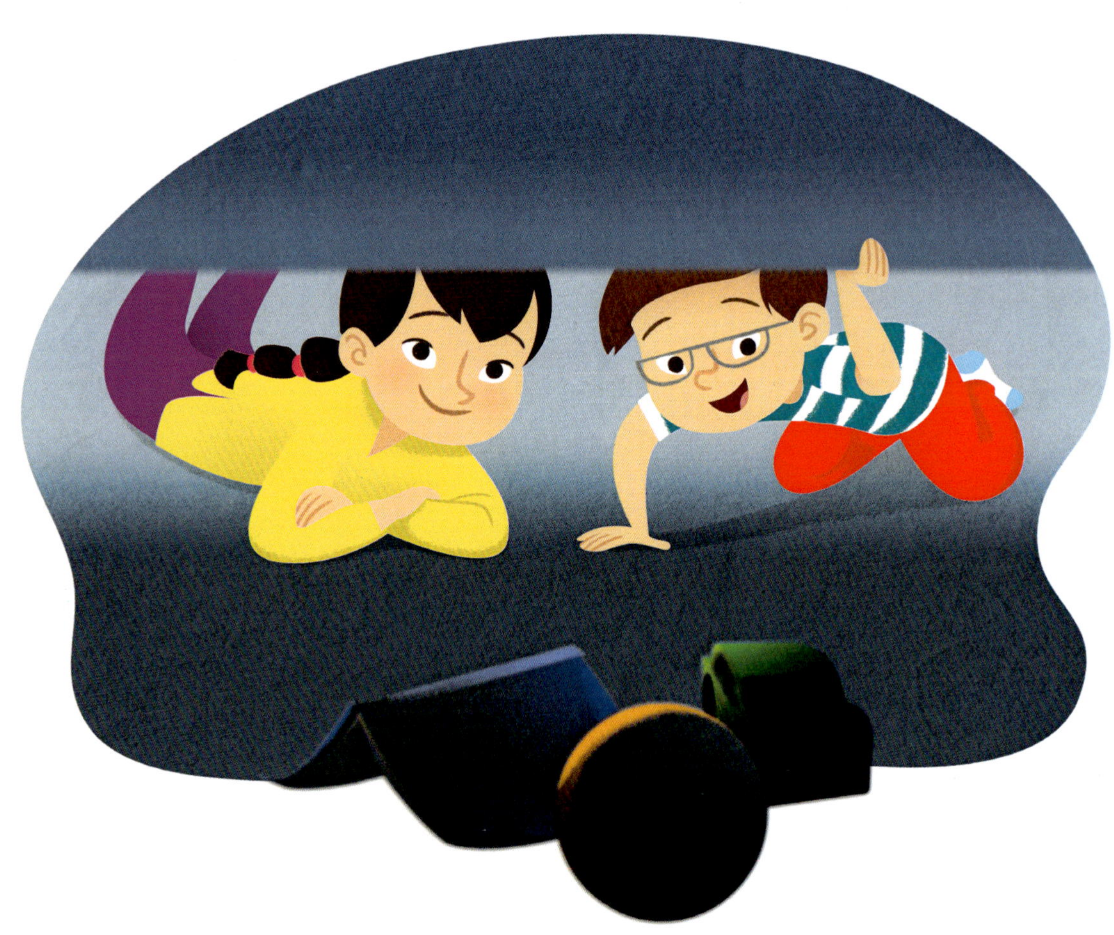

What do I see under my bed?

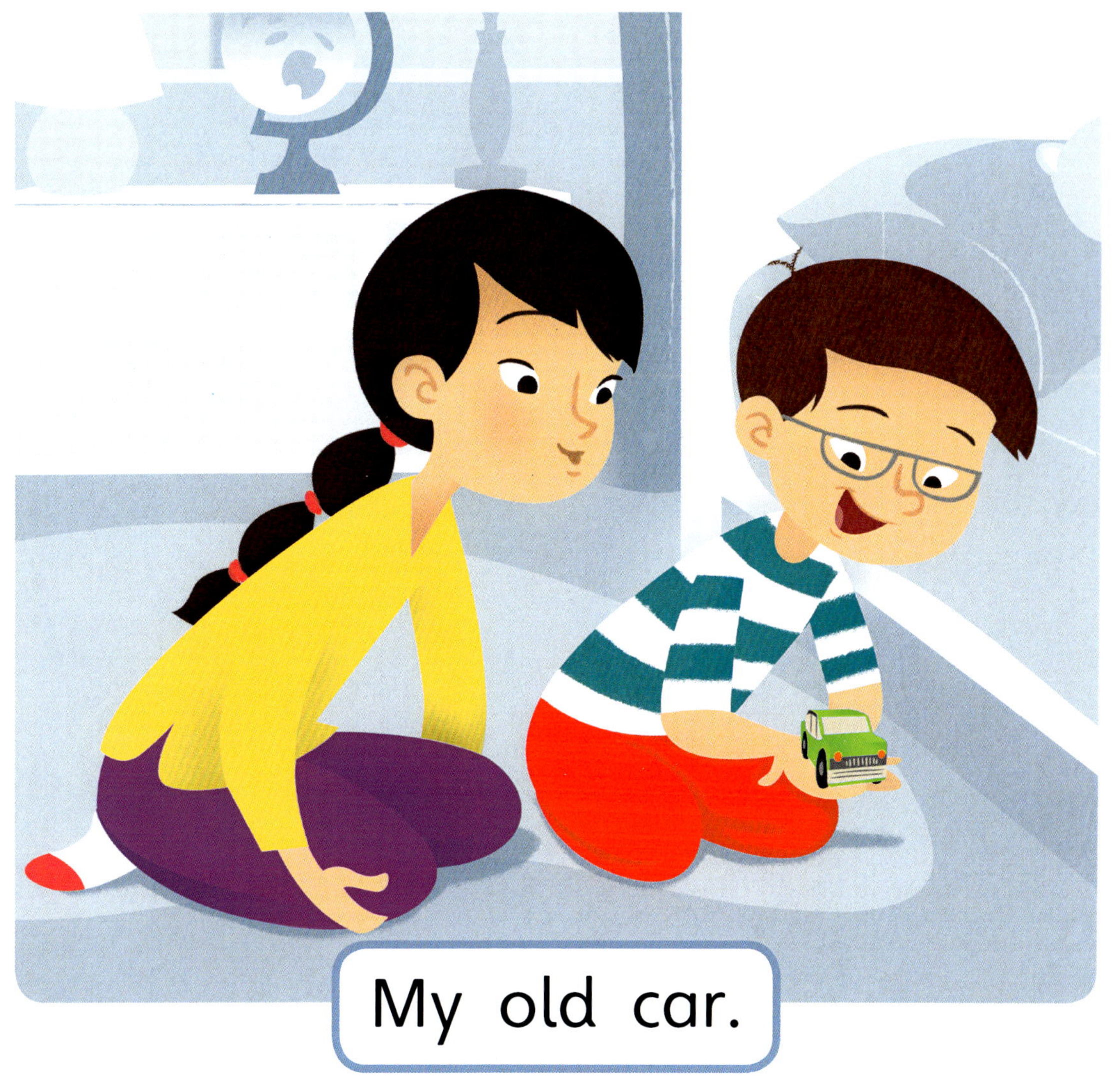

My old car.

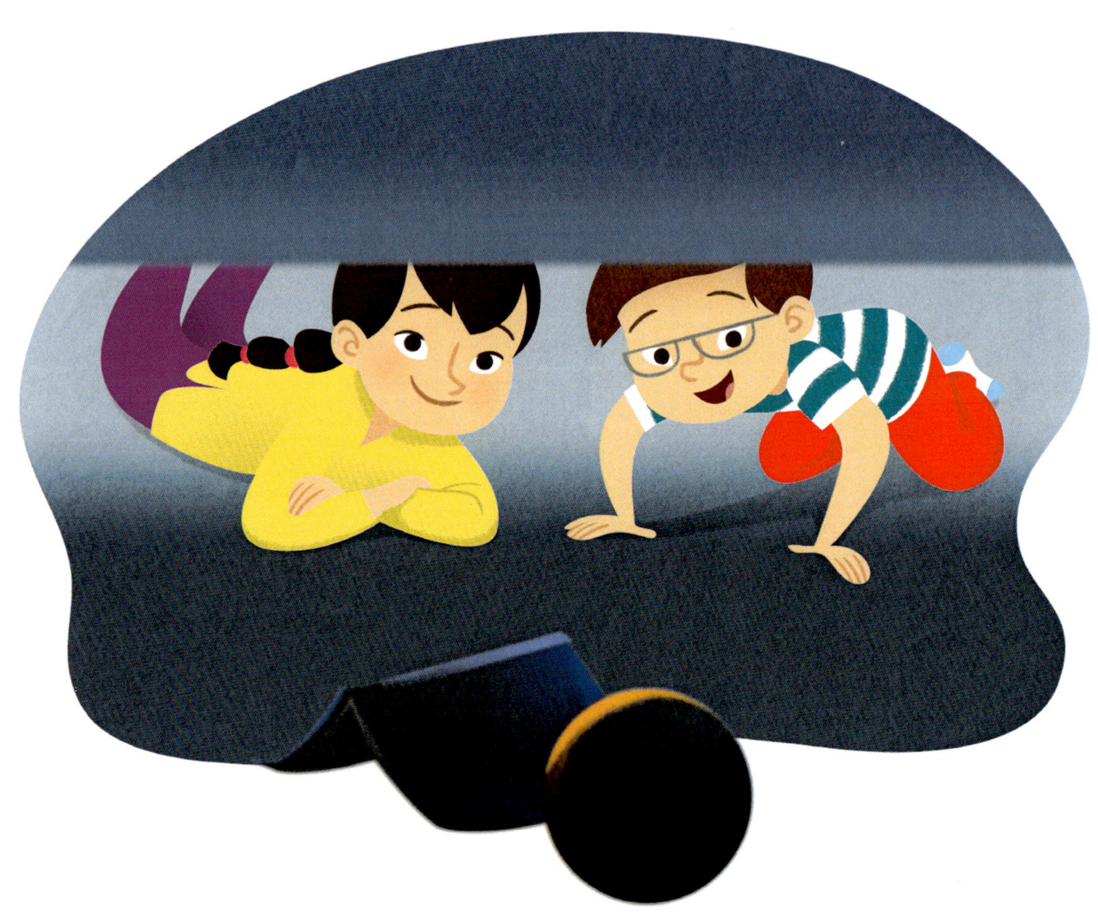

What do I see under my bed?

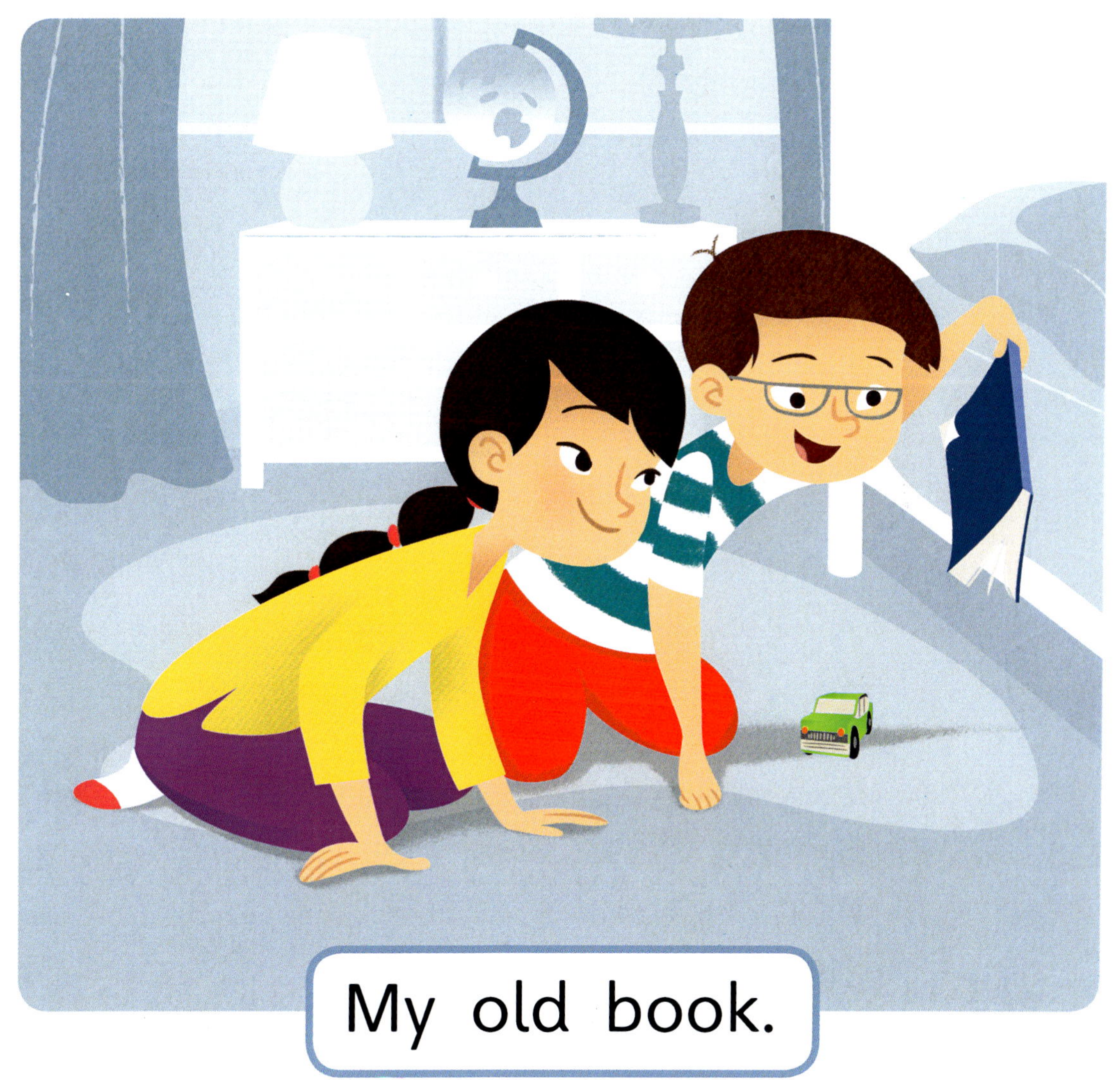

My old book.

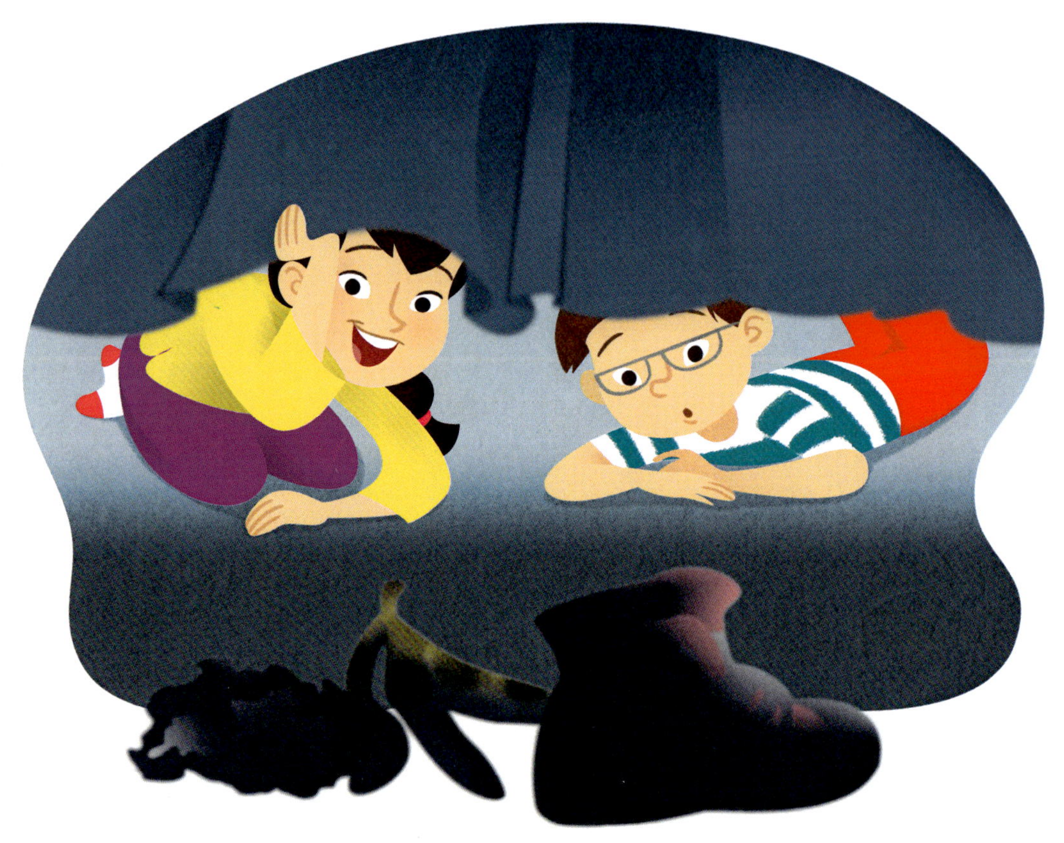

What do I see under *my* bed?

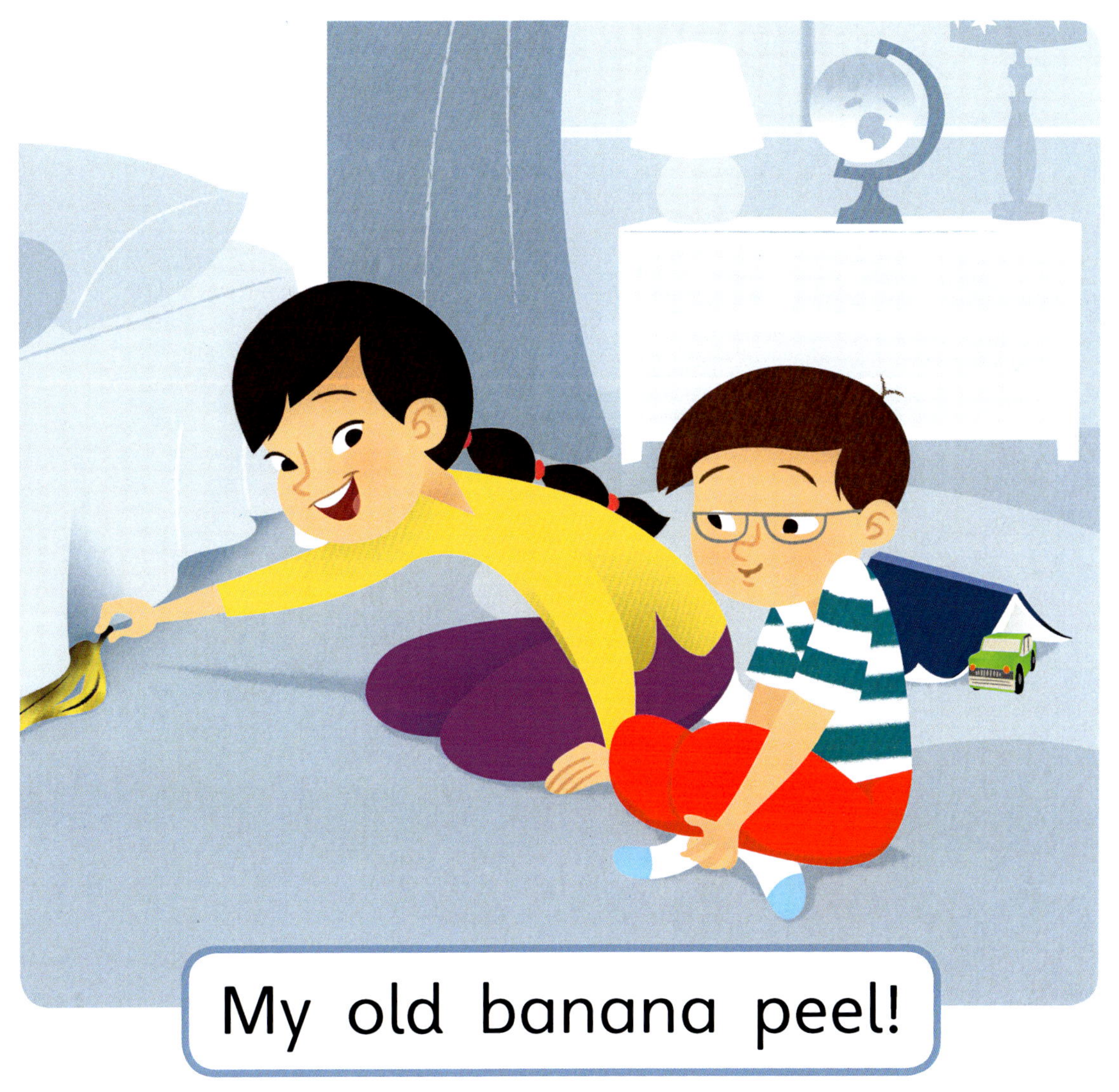

My old banana peel!

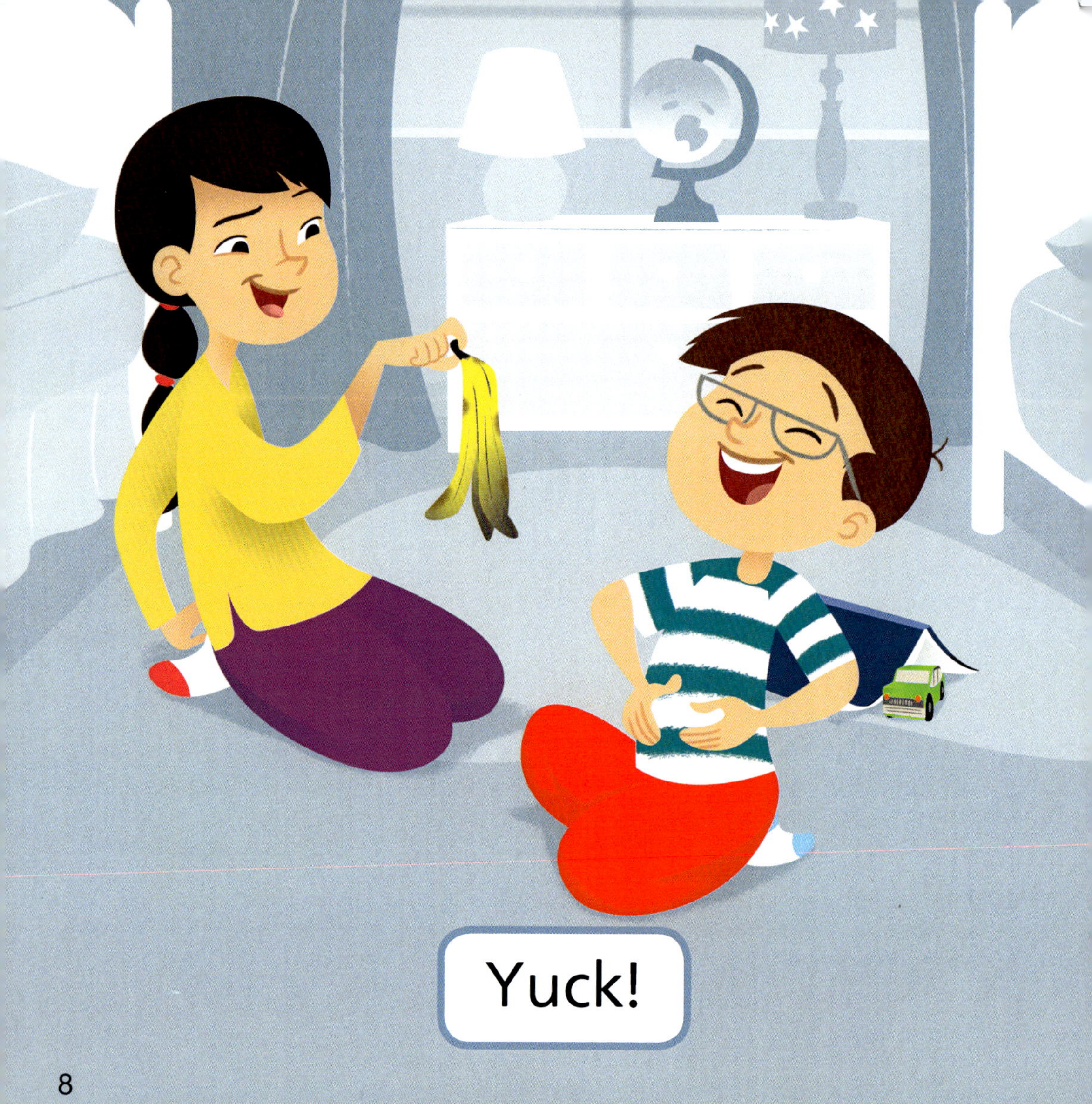

Yuck!